The Little
Wine
Steward

Pierre Petel

The Little Wine Steward

An international guide to harmonizing wine with food

Best Sellers Inc.

Toronto

English Translation Copyright © 1981, Bestsellers, Inc.

First published as *Le petit Sommelier* by Les Éditions du Jour Inc., Montreal, 1979.

Bestsellers, Inc.,
17 Queen Street East
Suite 439
Toronto, Canada M5C 1P9

Publisher: Glenn Edward Witmer
Translator: Alan Brown
Copy Editor: Greg Ioannou
Production Editor: Catherine Van Baren
Design: First Image/Michael Gray
Composition: Video Text Inc./Rupert Bisram
Painting on Front Cover: detail from "Nature morte au
    verre de vin" by Pierre Petel
Photograph of Painting: Suzanne Petel

Canadian Cataloguing in Publication Data

Petel, Pierre, 1920-
  The little wine steward

Translation of: Le petit sommelier.
Includes index.
ISBN 0-86507-002-4

1. Wine and wine making. 2. Menus. I. Title.

TP548.P4713   641.2′2   C81-094454-5

Printed and bound in Canada

CONTENTS

PREFACE

Some of my friends who fancy themselves in gastronomy (and can afford a very special but narrow choice) offer their guests nothing but great wines that are known world-wide; others cleverly manage to become veritable "subscribers" to three or four hush-hush vine growers whose more or less legible labels I find on their tables at every visit. Neither of these reproaches can be directed at Pierre Petel, who, in addition to the great vintages, remembers all those more modest wines that he has discovered and learned to appreciate. What a fund of knowledge! And what a cellar, beyond a doubt!

Pierre Petel will henceforth be your "cellarman," for he lists all the dishes of the classical cuisine—as well as certain famous preparations of foreign origin—and recommends a choice of wines appropriate to each.

It may be that, for your part, you would have made a slightly different choice in certain cases, for we should never forget that each person has his own tastes and preferences according to the season or even the mood of a day, but we must be grateful to Pierre Petel for the classification he has made and for all his felicitous suggestions.

With his pocket wine-steward I wish you a good appetite and a healthy thirst.

Odette Kahn
Internationally acclaimed food editor, journalist and Paris-based TV personality

Paris, *July 1979*.

INTRODUCTION

*Good wine stimulates our thoughts when
they are slow to come and rewards them
on arrival.*

During all my years as a writer on,
taster of and adviser in wines, most
of the questions people asked me
were not on the history of wine, or
vinification, or classification, or
vineyards, or vintage years, but
rather on the harmonizing of wine
with food. Even now, scarcely a
day goes by that someone doesn't
ask me what wines to serve with
such-and-such a preparation of
beef, lamb, veal or fish. I am wary
of the empirical reply that would
name a brand; I ask first about the
individual's tastes. Does he usually
like red wines, or white? I then
suggest to him a range of choices
within his tastes, warning, of
course, against certain heresies
that lie in wait for him.

Oh, I know the problems that these
questions pose, and the polemics
that can be started in an area as
vast and complex as the harmonies
of taste, in which subjectivity plays
such a major part. But I have never

found that the arts of the table are martial arts, and the argument always ends over a fine bottle whose demise on occasion leaves behind an undying memory.

How simple it would be if there were only so many ways of cooking a certain kind of fish, for example, or a certain cut of meat! No such luck. Take the tournedos of beef: we can count no less than 45 ways of preparing it (Arlésienne, bohémienne, Clamart, Colbert, Rossini, Talleyrand, Dubarry, forestière, MacMahon, Mirabeau, provençale, etc.) and I don't know how many sauces to accompany them (béarnaise, bordelaise, maître d'hôtel, bercy, choron, etc.). We can understand that a wine that goes perfectly with one of these recipes may be impossible with another; and we haven't even begun to mention boiled or braised or charcoal braised beef, rib steak and so on.

Well! For those who have no desire to explore the mysterious connections and agreements between wines and foods, it may be enough to know that beef, lamb, game and cheeses get along well with red wines, whether Bordeaux, Burgundies, or Côtes du Rhône; and that shellfish, veal and fish call for white wines. But there are those who are not satisfied with these simple postulates, who are constantly in search of subtle harmonies, want to hear fresh sounds and to extend to eating that desire for perfection which they apply to other areas of their lives. And isn't everyone trying endlessly to improve both his accomplishments and his tastes? And even himself?

This little pocket guide, then, is addressed to everyone, with the purpose, let it be said without pretentions, of admitting them to the very legitimate joys of eating well and drinking well. And, of course, to the knowledge that brings so much satisfaction, even if it is only the pleasure of sharing with friends the results of one's own research.

We will have occasion in this guide to recommend wines that are white or red, light or full-bodied, dry, semi-sweet or sweet, rosé or sparkling, with no indication of origin. On the next pages is a general table that may act as a reminder, allowing the reader to find his way through the multitude of wines that compete for his attention.

First, a word about the labels that appear in this guide: they were kindly made available by the wine merchants' representatives and are the only direct suggestions contained in this booklet. We tried to distribute them fairly and without —needless to say—any commercial involvement on our part, as a service to the reader.

Before we come to the main portion of the guide—the wine and food concordance—it should be mentioned that not all the wines referred to here are necessarily available at the same time and place, whether in Montreal, Chicago, New York or even Paris, but that they may turn up from time to time, according to the vagaries of politics and international agreements, or, simply, to the whim or fancy of importers.

The following table of 101 wines, while not exhaustive, illustrates the astonishing variety of white wines, dry, semi-sweet or sweet, of

red wines, light or robust, still
wines and wines sparkling or semi-
sparkling, available to our imagin-
ation and our knowing choice, to
grace those feasts of family or
ceremony that deserve their
presence.

Classifications of 101 Wines

	WHITE WINES	RED WINES	ROSÉ WINES	SEMI-SPARKLING	SPARKLING	LIGHT	ROBUST	DRY	SEMI-SWEET	SWEET
Aligoté	•					•		•		
Alsace	•					•				
Anjou	•	•	•	•	•				•	
Arbois	•	•			•	•	•	•		
Bandol		•					•			
Barbaresco		•				•				
Bardolino		•				•				
Barolo		•					•			
Barsac	•									•
Beaujolais		•				•				
Beaujolais grands crus		•					•			

	WHITE WINES	RED WINES	ROSÉ WINES	SEMI-SPARKLING	SPARKLING	LIGHT	ROBUST	DRY	SEMI-SWEET	SWEET	
Beaumes-de-Venise		•	•							•	
Bergerac	•	•				•		•	•		
Bikaver		•					•				
Blanquette de Limoux	•			•	•	•		•			
Bommes	•									•	
Bordeaux	•	•	•			•	•	•			
Bourgogne	•	•	•		•		•	•			
Bourgueil		•				•					
Cabernet d'Anjou			•					•			
Cahors		•					•				
Canon-Fronsac		•				•					
Carinena		•					•	•			
Chablis	•										
Champagne	•				•			•	•		
Chinon		•				•					
Châteauneuf-du-Pape		•					•				
Château-Grillet	•						•	•			
Chianti classico		•					•				

	WHITE WINES	RED WINES	ROSÉ WINES	SEMI-SPARKLING	SPARKLING	LIGHT	ROBUST	DRY	SEMI-SWEET	SWEET
Chusclan		•					•			
Clairette de Die	•			•	•			•	•	
Condrieu	•						•			
Corbières		•	•				•			
Cornas		•					•			
Corton		•					•			
Costières du Gard	•	•	•				•	•		
Coteaux du Layon	•									•
Coteaux du Tricastin	•	•	•				•	•		
Côtes du Lubéron		•				•				
Côtes de Provence	•	•	•				•			
Côte-Rôtie		•					•			
Côtes du Ventoux		•				•				
Coulée-de-Serrant	•							•	•	•
Crépy	•					•				
Crozes-Hermitage		•					•			

	WHITE WINES	RED WINES	ROSÉ WINES	SEMI-SPARKLING	SPARKLING	LIGHT	ROBUST	DRY	SEMI-SWEET	SWEET
Dâo	•	•					•			
Dolcetto		•				•				
Dôle		•					•			
Entre-Deux-Mers	•					•				
Ermitage*		•					•			
Fendant	•						•			
Fitou		•					•			
Frascati	•					•				
Gaillac	•	•	•	•	•		•	•	•	•
Gamza		•				•				
Gigondas		•					•			
Graves	•	•					•			
Gros-Plant	•					•				
Hemus	•									•
Hermitage**		•					•			
Hymetus	•					•				
Irancy		•				•				
Irouléguy	•	•					•	•		

*Also spelled with an "H"

**Also written without an "H"

	WHITE WINES	RED WINES	ROSÉ WINES	SEMI-SPARKLING	SPARKLING	LIGHT	ROBUST	DRY	SEMI-SWEET	SWEET
Lirac			•							
Lunel (Muscat de)	•									•
Mâcon	•	•					•			
Madiran		•					•			
Marsala	•							•	•	•
Merlot		•				•				
Meursault	•						•	•		
Minervois		•	•			•				
Mireval (Muscat de)	•									•
Monbazillac	•									•
Montrachet	•						•			
Moselle	•						•		•	
Neuchâtel	•	•	•	•		•		•		
Orvieto	•						•			
Passe-tout-grain		•					•			
Pécharmant		•				•				
Pouilly-Fuissé	•						•			
Pouilly-Fumé	•						•			
Rivesaltes (muscat de)	•									•

	WHITE WINES	RED WINES	ROSÉ WINES	SEMI-SPARKLING	SPARKLING	LIGHT	ROBUST	DRY	SEMI-SWEET	SWEET
Quarts-de-Chaume	•									•
Riesling	•						•			
Rioja	•	•				•	•			
Sancerre	•						•			
Sangre de Toro		•					•			
Sauternes	•									•
Savennières	•						•			
Savoie	•					•				
Saint-Joseph		•					•			
Saint-Peray	•				•		•			
Saint-Pourçain	•					•				
Soave	•					•				
Tavel			•				•			
Tokay (Pinot gris)	•						•			
Tokay (Hongrie)	•									•
Valdepenas	•	•				•				
Valpolicella		•				•				
Verdicchio	•						•			
Vin vert	•			•		•				
Zinfandel		•					•			

May I be allowed, before ending this long preamble, to recall a few elementary rules that Raymond Dumay, in his *Guide du Vin* (Stock), has assembled in the form of ten commandments:

1/No great sweet wines with dark meat or game;
2/No great red wines with fish or shellfish;
3/Dry white wines precede red wines;
4/Light wines precede robust wines;
5/Chilled wines precede wines served at room temperature;
6/Wines should be served in ascending order of excellence;
7/To each dish, its own wine (this is the purpose of the present guide);
8/Serve wines in their best season;
9/Separate your wines by a drink of water;
10/A great wine should not have to solo throughout a meal.

One last remark: you will find the name of a dish occasionally followed by a brief description in brackets. Examples:

SAUTE OF VEAL "MARENGO"
—Sauté de veau "marengo"
(sauce with tomatoes, garlic, crayfish)

LOBSTER À L'AMERICAINE—
Homard à l'Américaine
(onion, tomato, garlic)

It's obvious that in these cases the words in brackets are not a list of all the ingredients of the dish but rather basic elements of it or dominant tastes (to save looking them up in a culinary dictionary), which are mentioned as a clue to our reasons for choosing the wine that goes with them.

Now I shall let the wine speak for itself; it will be our best guide throughout this little treatise on harmony. "Wine," said Claudel, "the teacher of taste, by training us in the practice of inner alertness, becomes a liberator of the mind, the illuminator of intelligence."

I. SOUPS

"Well-doctored dishes with un-doctored wines!"

In principle, wine is not served with soups, unless, of course, soup is the "meal in itself," as in the case of goulash or bouillabaisse. But we know about principles: "Lean on them a little," someone said, "They'll give way!"

We can always drink water, perhaps sherry, or Madeira, or a dry port. If a light wine was served as an aperitif—a Beaujolais or a wine from the Jura—we can finish it off with the soup, drinking it from the glass or pouring it into the soup or consommé, which is called in French "faire chabrol" (or "chabrot"), an expression from the Limousin region. Or, one can steal a start on the wine that follows, a practice known for some reason as "le coup du docteur," or the doctor's trick.

The soup wine generally harmonizes with that of the next course.

SHRIMP BISQUE—Bisque de crevettes
>   robust whites—Tokay, Graves

CRAYFISH BISQUE—Bisque d'écrevisses
>   robust whites—Château-Grillet, Verdicchio

LOBSTER BISQUE—Bisque de homard
>   whites—Provence, Pouilly-Fuissé, Aligoté, Corton-Charlemagne, Rully
>   sweet whites—Barsac

SCAMPI BISQUE—Bisque de langoustines
>   Aligoté, Muscadet sur lies, Rully

BEET SOUP (BORSCHT)—
Potage Bortsch
(sour cream, beets)
reds—Graves, Pécharmant

FISH SOUP, PROVENCE
STYLE—Bouillabaisse
dry whites—Muscadet, Jurançon, Bandol, Cassis*, Entre-Deux-Mers, rosés from Provence, Vin de sables

CHOWDER
port, Madeira, sherry, Tokay d'Alsace (Pinot gris), Côtes-du-Rhône

CONSOMMÉ
port, Madeira, sherry (or the wine of the following course)

GARBURE
(bread, vegetables)
robust reds
Corbières, Dôle, Hermitage

GAZPACHO
rosés, Manzanilla, sangria

SWALLOW'S NEST SOUP—
Potage au nid d'hirondelle
tea, Champagne nature (still white Champagne)

*In all our wine harmonies this refers to the white wine from Provence, not the liqueur from Burgundy.

ONION SOUP—Soupe à l'oignon gratinée
    light reds
    Beaujolais, Bergerac
    Lubéron

CLAM SOUP—Soupe aux clams (clovisses)
    whites—Provence, Listel
    gris, Pouilly-Fuissé

VEGETABLE SOUP—soupe aux légumes

rosés, reds—Médoc,
Beaujolais, Provence (those
higher in alcohol content),
Vin de sables

COUNTRY SOUP—Soupe paysanne

local reds (Corbières,
Minervois, Cahors)

FISH SOUP—Soupe de poisson

whites, Entre-Deux-Mers,
rosés from Provence, Tavel

VELOUTE OF AVOCADO— Velouté d'avocat

great Burgundies
white—Chassagne-
Montrachet

II. HORS-D'OEUVRE

*A fig for the flagon
if the wine is strong.*
A. de Musset

1—IN GENERAL
a) COLD

> dry whites—Alsace, Africa,
> Spain, Italy
> semi-dry wines, rosés

> (in summer)
> Côtes-de-Provence, Sancerre,
> Vinho Verde (Portugal),
> Vouvray (well cooled),
> Faisca, Mateus

b) HOT

> Aligoté, Côtes-de-Provence,
> Sancerre

2—IN PARTICULAR

GARLIC BREAD—Pain à l'ail
> whites and rosés from
> Provence, blanc de Cassis,
> sangria

**CHITTERLING SAUSAGES—
Andouillettes**
> Beaujolais, Coteaux du

Tricastin, Chinon, Bourgueil, Brouilly, Mâcon

SMOKED EEL—Anguilles fumées
>
> beer, Akvavit, vodka, Moselle

ANTIPASTO
> *(Italian cold cuts, salami, sausages, cooked ham)*
> Soave, Muscadet Sèvre-et-Maine, Bardolino, Valpolicella, Chinon

ARTICHOKES—Artichauts
> California "Chablis"

ASPARAGUS—Asperges
Anjou, sweet Saumur,
Sauternes, Pouilly-Fuissé

COLD MEAT PLATE—Assiette anglaise
Chablis, Graves, Muscadet,
Dâo, Pinot Chardonnay
Niagara

STUFFED EGGPLANT
Sangre de Toro, Zinfandel

AVOCADOS WITH SEAFOOD—Avocats aux fruits de mer
Ermitage, white Alsace,
rosés, California Cabernet

AVOCADOS VINAIGRETTE
sherry

CANNELLONI
Côtes-de-Provence,
Valpolicella, Fleurie, Saint-
Amour

CAVIAR
(toast)
Champagne (brut, or drier
than extra-dry), Chablis,
Pouilly-Fuissé, Muscadet,
Vouvray (perhaps a Graves;
some prefer Sauternes or
iced vodka)

ON MARRYING A DISH WITH ITS WINE

The same dish can be accompanied
by different wines, depending on
whether it is served as the only
dish in a family meal or as an
appetizer at an official reception; or
according to whether it is served at
noon or in the evening, or on a
winter day as opposed to a sunlit
summer day in a festive garden.

For example, it would be an error to
serve as an appetizer a fish requir-
ing a sweet wine, followed by dark
meat (game or venison) with red
wine; or a matelote with red wine

followed by a chicken in sauce with white wine.

These are questions of sequence for optimal tasting, called for by the palate itself. For it's the palate that dictates the order in the parade, insisting that vinaigrette sauce is wine's worst enemy; that wine dislikes ice cream, and chocolate mousse, and the acidity of certain fruits.

CHARCUTERIE
(cold pork preparations, sausages, other prepared meats)
rosés, Tavel, Gigondas, light red Bordeaux—Passe-tout-grain, Languedoc, Anjou, Saumur, Jura, Cahors, Côtes du Ventoux, Côtes du Lubéron, Madiran, Coronas (Spain), Seibel (Niagara)

MARINATED HERRING—
Hareng mariné
ordinary reds, dry sherry,
Alsace, Riesling, Dutch gin,
Akvavit, Dâo

PIZZA
red wines (Italian, Spanish,
Australian)

SARDINES
dry white wines

SAUSAGES
light red wines—Médoc,
Beaujolais
dry white wines—Muscadet;
rosés
also Vouvray, California
Pinot Noir

III. ENTRÉES
(APPETIZERS)

Give me not kisses from the loveliest lass
But those that moisten in a wine-filled glass!
Anonymous, eighteenth century

ASPIC OF FOIE GRAS—Aspic de foie gras

> white wines—Meursault,
> Château-Grillet,
> Banyuls;
> red wines—Saint-Emilion,
> Pomerol
> Sauternes, Quarts-de-Chaume,
> sparkling Champagne

ASPIC OF HAM—Aspic de jambon

> red wines, Anjou, rosés

ASPIC OF SCAMPI—Aspic de langoustines

> Muscadet, Gewürztraminer,
> Monbazillac

ASPIC OF GAME—Aspic de gibier

(Woodcock, venison, hare, partridge)
   robust red wines—Côte
   de Nuits, Hermitage,
   Châteauneuf-du-Pape,
   Cahors, Saint-Emilion,
   Pomerol

SNACKS—Casse-croûte
   (rillettes, sausages, mortadella, galantines)
   dry white wines—Muscadet
   rosés, Vouvray
   light red wines—Médoc,
   Beaujolais

MUSHROOMS (see also
MORELS)**—Cèpes**
   (cooked with grated cheese or sauce)

in general, the same wine as
for the entrée
great white wines—Graves,
Meursault, Montrachet,
Cérons, Vouvray

CHILI CON CARNE
beer, Egri, Bikaver, Tavel

CHOP SUEY
tea, beer, sake (hot), Chinon

STUFFED CABBAGE—Chou farci
local red wines, Fleurie;
white wines, Chassagne-
Montrachet

CAULIFLOWER AU GRATIN—Chou-fleur au gratin
Aligoté, Bourgueil, Chinon,
red Bordeaux

SAUERKRAUT—Choucroute
beer, Gewürztraminer,
Riesling, Champagne nature
(still white Champagne)

COOKED DELICATESSEN MEATS—Cochonnailles
(blood pudding, head-cheese, heart, liver)
>Costières-du-Gard, Corbières, Lubéron, Ventoux, Tricastin, Côtes-du-Rhône, Beaujolais, Julienas, Brouilly

CRÊPES

BRITTANY STYLE—Crêpe Bretonne
>cider, Muscadet

WITH EGGS AND CHEESE—aux oeufs et fromage
>cider

WITH ROQUEFORT—au Roquefort
>Costières-du-Gard
>Saint-Pourçain red
>Vin de sables

FROGS' LEGS—Cuisses de grenouille
Aligoté

FROGS' LEGS WITH GARLIC— Cuisses de grenouille Provençale
Mâcon white, Pouilly-Fuissé, Tokay (Alsace)

EGG ROLLS (See CHOP SUEY)

SNAILS—Escargots
Condrieu, Beaujolais, Côtes-du-Rhône, Mâcon, Meursault, Graves, Ermitage, Médoc

STUFFED VINE LEAVES
rosé from Provence, robust Côtes-du-Rhône reds

PORK AND BEANS—Fèves au lard
Bordeaux supérieur, Pécharmant, Saint-Amour

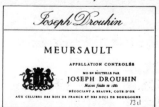

FOIE GRAS
(fattened goose or duck liver paste)

(as an appetizer)
Blanc de blancs Champagne, Loupiac, Sainte-Croix-du-Mont, Gewürztraminer, Muscadet, Meursault, Montrachet
or semi-dry or sweet wines—Alsace, Graves,
or German: Spätlese, Auslese

(as an after-course)
great reds or whites on the sweet side—Beaune, Pommard, Chambertin, Hermitage, Châteauneuf-du-Pape, Sauternes, Coulée-de-Serrant, Monbazillac, port

FONDUE SAVOYARDE
Fendant du Valais, semi-sparkling Neuchâtel

GNOCCHI
(pasta, cream, eggs)
robust reds, rosés (Lirac), or light red Bordeaux

GOUGERE
(Burgundian pastry)
Aligoté, Rully

HOT DOGS
Beaujolais, beer

LASAGNA A LA BOLOGNESE
Bardolino

MACARONI AU GRATIN
light reds—Crépy, Chianti

MELON
port, sherry, sweet Madeira,
Meursault, Sauternes

MORELS—Morilles
light reds, second or third
growth Médoc, great Beaune
wines, Corton, Volnay,
Côte-Rôtie

SCRAMBLED EGGS—Oeufs brouillés
Bordeaux, Pouilly/Loire,
Sancerre, Graves

QUAIL EGGS IN ASPIC—Oeufs de caille en aspic
Alsace and Loire wines,
Beaujolais

BACON AND EGGS—Oeufs au plat et bacon

As for scrambled eggs on page 37.

EGGS IN FISH STEW—Oeufs en meurette

(cooked with wine)

Beaujolais-villages (this, with the quail eggs above, is an exception to the rule which normally bars red wines with eggs)

EGGS-GENERAL—Oeufs simples

whites—Entre-deux-Mers, Graves, Ermitage, Burgundy (white), Aligoté
fish wines—Côtes-du-Rhône, Alsace, Pouilly-Fuissé

EGGS HAUTE CUISINE
     Vouvray, Cérons (sweet)

QUAIL EGGS, REMOULADE SAUCE—Oeufs de caille remoulade
     (hot mustard, vinegar, capers)
     whites—Riesling, rosés

PLAIN OMELETTE—Omelette simple
     ordinary reds—Côtes-du-Rhône

OMELETTE GRATINEE
     Sancerre, Aligoté, Orvieto
     light red wines

TRUFFLE AND MUSHROOM OMELETTE—Omelette aux truffes et champignons
     Great wines—Saint-Emilion,
     Médoc, Pomerol,
     Chambertin,
     Romanée, Vougeot

HAM OMELETTE—Omelette au jambon
     Chinon, Bourgueil, Anjou,
     Beaujolais

CHEESE OMELETTE—Omelette au fromage
     rosés—Anjou,
     Beaujolais

PAELLA
Côtes-de-Provence, Rioja
or Penedès whites,
Tavel

PAELLA CATALAN—Paella catalane
*(clams, chicken, pork,
tomatoes)*
white or red Spanish wines,
Vina Sol, Coronas

PAELLA OF VALENCIA—Paella valencienne
(chicken, rabbit, pork)
Côtes-de-Provence, Rioja
or Penedès white, Tavel

GAME PATE—Pâté de gibier (venison)
robust reds—Ermitage,
Châteauneuf-du-Pape,
Saint-Emilion

(quail)
   light reds

COUNTRY PATE (coarse-grained)—Pâté de campagne
   earthy wines (Corbières
   Minervois, Roussillon),
   Burgundy, Pouilly-Fuissé
   whites—Hermitage

PISSALADIERE
   *(flan tart filled with onions,
   anchovy fillets, black olives)*
   rosés from Provence

COLD POTATOES—Pommes de terre froides
   (salads)
   all dry, perfumed whites

QUICHE
   whites, semi-dry—Loire

and Bordeaux, Alsace,
Riesling,
Gewürztraminer

RACLETTE
(Cheese fondue from Valais)
Fendant, Savoie (Crépy,
Seyssel),
white Mâcon,
Chablis, Gros-Plant

SPAGHETTI
Italian wines, Chianti,
Valpolicella; light Bordeaux
Vin Nouveau (Niagara-on-
the-Lake)

SPARE RIBS—Travers de porc
Cabernet d'Anjou,
Monbazillac,
Fleurie

TERRINE OF LIVER—Terrine de foie
full-bodied whites,
Burgundies,
Condrieu

TRUFFLES—Truffes
all great wines

VOL-AU-VENT (Pastry shell with filling)
(includes bouchées à la reine and quenelles)

Anjou, Provence, Condrieu, Quincy, Riesling, sweet and semi-dry wines

About wine temperatures:

Sparkling wines are served in an ice-bucket	*5-6°C*	*41-42°F*
Sweet white wines	*7-8°C*	*44-46°F*
Champagne	*8-9°C*	*46-48°F*
White and rosé wines	*10°C*	*50°F*
Light red wines	*10-15°C*	*50-59°F*
Robust, full-bodied wines	*15-20°C*	*59-68°F*

IV
CRUSTACEANS
AND
SHELLFISH

*Drink wine and
speak Latin!*

1. IN GENERAL
a) RAW

Sylvaner, Riesling, Moselle,
Pouilly-Fuissé, Pouilly-Fumé,
Sancerre, Muscadet, Sèvre-
et-Maine, Loire, Graves,
Entre-deux-Mers, Mâcon
blanc, Aligoté, Tavel, Rosés
from Provence, Chardonnay
(Californian)

b) BOILED, FRIED
full-bodied whites, white
Ermitage

2. IN PARTICULAR
**SCALLOP SAINT-JACQUES—
Coquille St-Jacques**
(in cream)
white Burgundy
Pouilly-Vinzelle, German

wines, Qualitätswein,
Barsac, Sauternes, Anjou
(semi-dry), Vouvray

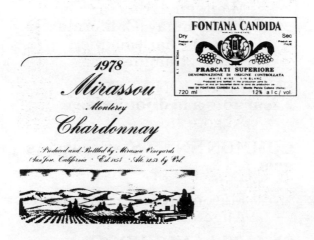

SCALLOPS ST. JACQUES—
Coquille St-Jacques
(grated cheese)
Riesling, Muscadet, Chablis,
Entre-deux-Mers, Saumur
blanc, Bordeaux red (light),
Frascati,
Orvieto, California Chenin

CRAYFISH—Écrevisse à la
nage
(in aromatic bouillon)
Muscadet, Vouvray, Quincy,
Jura, Arbois (white),
Verdicchio, Frascati, or light
reds, California Chardonnay

SNAILS BURGUNDY— Escargots de Bourgogne
    Pouilly-Fuissé, Chablis,
    Montagny, Aligoté,
    Chardonnay (California),
    Corton-Charlemagne,
    Gewürztraminer

SNAILS DIJON STYLE— Escargots à la dijonnaise
    Aligoté

COMMON SNAILS—Escargots gris
    (small)
        Mâcon, Muscadet, Sylvaner,
        Aligoté

SNAILS LANGUEDOC— Escargots à la languedocienne
    (mushrooms, egg plant, tomatoes)
        Clairette, Cassis (Provence),
        Côtes-de-Provence,
        Coteaux du Languedoc

DEEP-FRIED SEAFOOD— Friture
    robust whites

SEAFOOD GRATINE—Fruits de mer gratinés
    yellow wines (Jura),
    Châteauneuf-du-Pape
    (white),

Meursault, rosés from
Provence, vintage
Champagne

LOBSTER A L'AMERICAINE—
Homard à l'américaine
(Armoricaine)
(onions, tomatoes, garlic)
strong reds—Châteauneuf-
du-Pape,
strong rosés—Tavel,
dry or sweet whites—Corton-
Charlemagne, Montrachet,
California Chardonnay,
Graves, Sauternes, Château
d'Yquem

LOBSTER NEWBURG—
Homard Newburg
(sweet cream, mayonnaise)
great whites, dry or semi-
sweet—Ermitage, Sauternes;
Madeira, Port

LOBSTER THERMIDOR—
Homard Thermidor
(Bechamel sauce)
great whites, dry or semi-
sweet

LOBSTER CARDINAL—
Homard Cardinal
great whites, dry or semi-
sweet

OYSTERS—Huîtres
white Burgundy, Chablis,
Pouilly-Fuissé, Alsace,
Riesling, Muscadet, Clairette
du Languedoc, Entre-deux-
Mers, Graves, Chavignol
Sancerre, Pouilly-Fumé,
Condrieu,
Champagne;
light reds served chilled—
Beaujolais,
Valpolicella;
a classic: Chablis

SCAMPI A L'AMERICAINE—
Langoustines à l'américaine
Tavel

SCAMPI SWEET AND SOUR—
Langoustines à l'aigre-douce
tea, beer, rosé wines—

Coteaux du Layon,
Rivesaltes,
Barsac, Saint-Amour

**MUSSELS MARINIERE—
Moules marinières**
dry whites—Graves,
Sancerre,
Condrieu, Arbois,
Champagne

V. FISH

Deep in wine a soul lies hidden.

Théodore de Banville

1—IN GENERAL

a) LEAN FISH
(turbot, sole, ray, mackerel, cod, perch)

Chablis, Pouilly-Fuissé, Sancerre, Mosel, California "Chablis"

b) SEMI-LEAN FISH
(trout)

Pouilly-Fumé, Graves, white Côtes-du-Rhône, Condrieu, Saint-Joseph

c) FATTY FISH
(tuna, sturgeon, salmon, herring, sea-pike, eel)

sweet whites—Anjou
great dry whites—Meursault, Chassagne-Montrachet

2—IN PARTICULAR

FRIED EEL—Anguille frite
water, beer, dry sherry,
Muscadet, Gros-Plant,
Mâcon (white), Riesling

(in matelote or fish sauce)
reds—Saint-Nicolas-de-
Bourgueil, Saint-Emilion

*Château d'Yquem, or the extravagance of
perfection. The chief cellarman of this
winery is said to be the "uncrowned king
of France...."*

César Mellot · Conseiller du Roy en 1698

Domaine La Moussière

SANCERRE

APPELLATION SANCERRE CONTROLÉE

Mis en bouteilles par Maison Mellot
à Sancerre (Cher)

ALPHONSE MELLOT
Propriétaire Récoltant . SANCERRE

SEA PERCH AND BRILL—
Bar, Barbue
> *(grilled or "à l'amiral,"*
> *poached, Nantua sauce)*
>> Mercurey, Hermitage (white),
>> Chablis, Montrachet,
>> Meursault or Sauternes

BRANDADE OF COD—
Brandade de morue
> *(garlic, oil, lemon)*
>> rosés—Côtes-de-Provence,
>> Rhine wines

PIKE AU BEURRE BLANC—
Brochet au beurre blanc
>> Muscadet, Anjou, Vouvray,
>> Saumur, Sancerre, Chablis,
>> Mâcon, Pouilly-Fuissé,
>> Alsace, Graves,
>> Château-Grillet;

traditional and unanimous choice: Sèvre-et-Maine muscadet

STUFFED CARP IN RED WINE—Carpe farcie au vin rouge

whites—Mâcon, Traminer, rosés of Provence, light Bordeaux

LAMPREY STEW BORDELAISE—Civet de lamproie bordelaise

red—Graves

SALMON STEAK BEARNAISE—Darne de saumon béarnaise

(shallots, tarragon, vinegar, egg)

Sancerre, Château-Grillet, Corton-Charlemagne, California Riesling

DORADO—Dorade
(or Daurade or Doré)
> whites and rosés of Provence,
> chilled white Bordeaux,
> Pouilly-Fuissé

FRIED SMELTS—Eperlans
frits
> whites—Anjou, dry or sweet
> Jurançon,
> Riesling

WHITING—Merlan
> Anjou, Chablis,
> Pouilly-Fuissé

COD WITH GARLIC—Morue à
l'ail
> Mâcon white,
> Gewürztraminer,
> blanc de blancs of Provence

SALMON MOUSSELINE—
Saumon mousseline
> *(whipped cream)*
> Sauternes, Château d'Yquem

FISH PATE—Pâté de poisson
> *(in jelly)*
> any dry, white wine;
> reds—Beaune, Moulin-à-Vent,
> Médoc

FISH AU GRATIN—Poisson au
gratin
> Rully, Seyssel (Savoie),

Sylvaner, Riesling (Niagara)

GRILLED FISH MEUNIERE— Poisson grillé meunière
(cod, eels, tuna, perch)
Moselle, Rhine, Sancerre

FISH POACHED IN RED WINE—Poisson poché au vin rouge
same wine as used for cooking, or Fleurie, Saint-Amour

FISH, ANY ELABORATE PREPARATION—Poisson très cuisiné
(rich sauces)
Alsace Tokay, Montrachet, Meursault, Pouilly-Fumé, Chavignol, Montlouis, Graves, great growths (such as Carbonnieux, Chevalier, Olivier), Sauternes, Barsac

FISH IN SAUCE—Poisson en sauce

(fish dumplings, pike, sole)
dry whites—Chablis,
Montrachet,
Corton-Charlemagne;
semi-sweet whites—Anjou,
Saumur;
sweet whites

FISH WITH HOLLANDAISE SAUCE—Poisson sauce hollandaise

(lemon, egg yolk)
Graves, Alsace, Montagny

SALMON—Saumon

whites—Loire, Côtes-de-
Bourg, Bordeaux

LA ROMANÉE SAINT·VIVANT

APPELLATION CONTRÔLÉE

MIS EN BOUTEILLE AU DOMAINE
CHARLES NOELLAT
PROPRIÉTAIRE-RÉCOLTANT A VOSNE-ROMANÉE (CÔTE D'OR)

PRODUCE OF FRANCE

Agent exclusif : **M. Robert PEIDES**

13,5% Alc. / Vol.   730 ml

COLD SALMON-MAYONNAISE—Saumon froid-mayonnaise
  Champagne, Vouvray

SOLE, POACHED—Sole pochée
  great white burgundies

SOLE, GRILLED—Sole grillée
  Alsace, Loire (Sancerre, Muscadet, Pouilly-Fumé)

TROUT—Truite
  whites—Loire, Graves

SALMON TROUT—Truite saumonée
  great dry white wines; preference: Puligny-Montrachet

57

BLUE TROUT—Truite au bleu
*(served with Hollandaise sauce
or mayonnaise)*
    Sylvaner, Alsace, Chablis

**TROUT WITH ALMONDS—
Truite aux amandes**
    whites—Loire,
    Pouilly-Fuissé

**TROUT MEUNIERE—Truite
meunière**
    Alsace, white Burgundy

**POACHED TURBOT—Turbot
poché**
    Sauternes,
    preference: Pouilly-Fuissé

VI. MEATS

The man who does not transform the pleasures of the table into a delight of the mind is not a true gastronome.

Maurice des Ombiaux

A—BEEF

1—IN GENERAL

a) BEEF, ROAST OR GRILLED —Boeuf rôti, grillé

Pauillac, Saint-Estèphe,
Côte de Nuits, Beaune
Ermitage, Saint-Emilion
Pomerol, Graves (red),
Corbières, Minervois,
Barolo, Bardolino,
California Cabernet

b) BEEF ON THE SPIT (OVEN)—Boeuf à la broche au four

Gevrey-Chambertin
Vosne-Romanée, Vougeot,
Bordeaux, Cahors, Côte-Rôtie

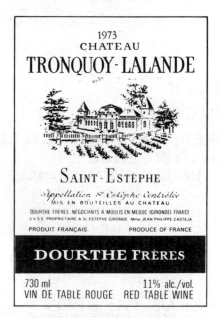

c) BOILED BEEF—Boeuf bouilli

> Côtes-du-Rhône, Bordeaux (light), Australian

2—IN PARTICULAR

BEEF BOURGUIGNON—
Boeuf bourguignon
Nuits-Saint-Georges,
Patrimonio (Corsica)

BEEF BOURGUIGNON
(with cloves)
Châteauneuf-du-Pape,
Chianti Classico

DAUBE OF BEEF—Boeuf en
daube
Cornas, Saint-Julien,
Madiran, Cahors

BEEF A LA MODE—Boeuf à la
mode
light reds, Beaujolais,
Chinon, Saumur, Anjou

BEEF PROVENCALE—Boeuf
provençale
(tomatoes, anchovies, olives)
Côtes-du-Rhône, Chianti

BEEF GOULASH—Boeuf goulache
> *(paprika, bacon, red wine)*
>> reds—Hungarian, Bulgarian, Cabernet

BEEF STROGANOFF—Boeuf Stroganov
> *(shallots, sweet cream)*
>> great Bordeaux (red)—
>> Margaux; Volnay
>> Hermitage
>> great white wines—Puligny
>> Montrachet
>> or:
>> Barolo, Amarone, Zinfandel

VINEYARDS ESTABLISHED 1825
1977
Sebastiani
FOUNDED AT THE END OF EL CAMINO REAL
NORTH COAST COUNTIES
ZINFANDEL
Unique "Bramble" Flavor
PRODUCED AND BOTTLED BY SEBASTIANI VINEYARDS
SONOMA, CALIFORNIA 95476, U.S.A.
ALC. 12½ % BY VOL. BONDED WINERY 876

About *Cahors:*

Ingres drank it for his health.

About *Bordeaux:*
Mother's milk for old men.
The wine of Richard II, la
Pompadour, Richelieu, Leo XIII,
Darwin, Queen Victoria.
Richelieu preferred Haut-Brion.
They called it "Richelieu's herb-
tea."

About *Burgundies:*
"The milk on which we have
nourished the best of our sons."
(Erasmus)

And *Champagne:*

The more of it we savour
The less our steps will waver.

**BEEF MIROTON—Boeuf
miroton**
   (a stew)
      dry whites;
      rosés;
      light reds: a chance to try
      "foreign" wines from
      Hungary, Spain, Italy,
      Portugal, Australia, Africa

BEEF WELLINGTON (in crust)—Boeuf Wellington (en croûte)

> Pauillac, Saint-Estèphe, Saint-Julien
> Châreauneuf-du-Pape

BEEFSTEAK, BBQ

> Bordeaux—Cahors, Côte-Rôtie

CARBONADES OF BEEF—Carbonades de boeuf

> *(fried, braised, onions)*
> beer

PORTERHOUSE STEAK—Châteaubriand

> Bordeaux supérieurs—Fitou, Savigny-les-Beaune, Echézeaux

CORNED BEEF
> local wines—Minervois,
> Corbières, Fitou, Ventoux,
> Lubéron etc.
> Gros-Plant (Nantais),
> Saumur,
> Chianti

GRILLED RIB OF BEEF—Côte de boeuf grillée
> Médoc, Cornas,
> Côte de Nuits, Côte de
> Beaune, Barolo, Australian
> Cabernet

RIB OF BEEF BOUQUETIERE (OVEN-COOKED)—Côte de boeuf bouquetière au four
> Côte-Rôtie, Volnay
> Châteauneuf-du-Pape,
> great Bordeaux

RIB OF BEEF CHARCUTIERE
—Côte de boeuf charcutière
(shallots, pickles)
Aligoté, Mâcon white,
chilled Saumur,
Entre-deux-Mers

STEAK—Entrecôte
reds—Corbières,
Costières-du-Gard,
Bardolino

STEAK BORDELAISE—
Entrecôte bordelaise
(mushrooms, shallots,
tarragon)
Bordeaux—Saint-Emilion,
Pécharmant,
Graves,
same red as used in sauce,
Haut-Brion, vodka

STEAK MARCHAND DE
VIN—Entrecôte marchand de
vin
(shallots, red wine)
Cahors, Saint-Amour

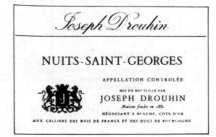

Joseph Drouhin

NUITS-SAINT-GEORGES

APPELLATION CONTROLÉE

MIS EN BOUTEILLE PAR
JOSEPH DROUHIN
Maison fondée en 1880
NÉGOCIANT A BEAUNE, CÔTE D'OR
AUX CELLIERS DES ROIS DE FRANCE ET DES DUCS DE BOURGOGNE

LES RICHEBOURG

APPELLATION CONTRÔLÉE

MIS EN BOUTEILLE AU DOMAINE

CHARLES NOELLAT

PROPRIÉTAIRE-RÉCOLTANT A VOSNE-ROMANÉE (CÔTE D'OR)

PRODUCE OF FRANCE

Agent exclusif : M. Robert PEIDES

13,5% Alc. Vol.   730 ml

BEEF FONDUE—Fondue bourguignonne
Burgundy,
Nuits-Saint-Georges,
Richebourg

BEEF TENDERLOIN FORESTIERE—Filet de boeuf forestière
(mushrooms)
Pommard, Saint-Emilion,
California Cabernet

BEEF TENDERLOIN EN BRIOCHE—Filet de boeuf en brioche
Châteauneuf-du-Pape

FILET MIGNON
>Bordeaux supérieurs
>Chassagne-Montrachet

GRAS DOUBLE
>*(first beef stomach, tripe)*
>reds—Graves, Chinon,
>Saint-Nicolas-de-Bourgueil,
>Chiroubles, Côte-Rôtie

HAMBURGER
>Chinon, Beaujolais,
>Corbières,
>Chianti, Zinfandel, Gamay,
>Niagara Beaujolais

TONGUE—langue
>dry whites

**TONGUE IN MADEIRA
SAUCE—Langue, sauce
Madère**
>Provence rosés, Madeira,
>white Ermitage

MIXED GRILL—Grillades
>local reds, Roussillon,
>Cahors,Fitou, Corbières,
>Costières-du-Gard,
>New York State wines

POT-AU-FEU
>*(boiled beef, chicken,
>vegetables)*
>the traditional Beaujolais, or
>Beaujolais-Villages

PEPPER STEAK—Steak au poivre

Médoc, Beaujolais,
Chiroubles,
Côte de Beaune, Madiran,
Côtes-du-Rhône, Hermitage

STEAK CHASSEUR
(mushrooms, tomatoes)

Saint-Emilion, Madiran

STEAK WITH FRENCH FRIES—Steak pommes frites

Beaujolais, Morgon, Fleurie

STEAK MIRABEAU
(anchovies)

Beaujolais, Cassis (white),
Tavel, Chusclan

STEAK TARTARE
(raw)
Beaujolais, Corsican red,
Bergerac, Valpolicella

STEAK TARTARE WITH ANCHOVIES—Avec anchois
Provence rosés, Chusclan,
Sancerre (white or red)

SUKIYAKI
tea, beer, sake (hot),
Chusclan, Cornas

MEDALLIONS OF TENDERLOIN BEEF (GRILLED)—Tournedos grillé
(mustard)
Bordeaux supérieurs,
Côtes-du-Rhône

TOURNEDOS ROSSINI
(foie gras, Madeira sauce)
Burgundy—La Tâche,
Patrimonio

OXTAIL—Queue de boeuf
Burgundy, Volnay,
Pomerol,
Barolo, Chianti,
Rioja Reserva,
Penedès,
whites—Corton-Charlemagne

How delightful, pretty jug,
How sweet thy sound (glug-glug,
glug-glug)

Molière

B—VEAL

1—IN GENERAL
light Bordeaux, German
wines

a) ROASTED, GRILLED
>Haut-Médoc, Pomerol,
Volnay, Savigny-les-Beaune,
Mercurey, Côtes-de-Provence,
Costières-du-Gard,
Bourgueil

b) IN SAUCE
>Graves, Mâcon-Viré,
Sancerre,
Beaujolais blanc, Quincy,
Orvieto, California
Sauvignon (white)

2—IN PARTICULAR

**VEAL BLANQUETTE—
Blanquette de veau**
>Loire, Muscadet,
Burgundy (white),
Mâcon (white)
light Bordeaux,
local red wines

CALF'S BRAINS—Cervelle
>Beaujolais, Chianti,
Pouilly-Fuissé

**CALF'S BRAINS AU BEURRE
NOIR—Cervelle au beurre noir**
>red Burgundies,
Saint-Emilion

**CALF'S BRAINS MEUNIERE—
Cervelle meunière**
>Bordeaux, Beaujolais,

Chianti, Rioja, Dâo,
Napa Valley Zinfandel;
Pouilly Fuissé

WINE AND COOKING

Wine is used in marinades,
enhanced with spices and some-
times with vinegar; in courts-
bouillons; and in sauces such as
Madeira, port, chasseur, Robert,
bordelaise and américaine.

It is not advisable to use great
wines for cooking, nor wines that
have turned sour or acid.

As the wine is heated the alcohol
evaporates and the bouquet
remains. Passe-tout-Grain is often
used by chefs, as is Mâcon red.

**VEAL SCALLOPS—Escalopes
de veau**
        young, fresh wines—
        Beaujolais,
        Saint-Amour,
        local red wines

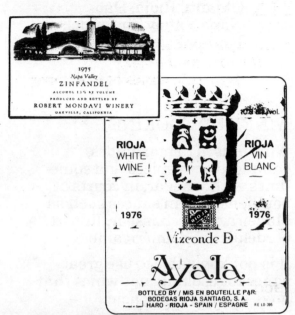

VEAL SCALLOPS "MILANAISE"—Escalopes "milanaise"
(fried, tomato sauce, mushrooms)
Provence rosés,
red Graves,
Valpolicella, Merlot,
Bardolino

VEAL SCALLOPS A LA NORMANDE—Escalopes à la normande
(fried, apple-sauce)
Loire, Sancerre

BREADED VEAL SCALLOPS (WIENER SCHNITZEL)—
Escalopes pannées "viennoise"
(lemon, anchovies)
dry white wines of the Loire;
rosés;
light reds

VEAL LIVER—Foie de veau
Bordeaux, Moulis,
Saint-Julien,
Burgundy, Nuits, Beaune,
Beaujolais, Morgon, Fleurie,
Brouilly, Mercurey,
Merlot (Italian), Zinfandel

LIVER AND BACON—Foie et bacon
Moulis, Listrac,
Saint-Estèphe,
Champigny, Sancerre rosé

KNUCKLE OF VEAL "JARDINIERE"—Jarret de veau "jardinière"
> white Anjou,
> Bourgueil

VEAL MEDALLIONS— Médaillons de veau
> robust whites,
> light reds,
> Bandol

BRAISED KERNEL OF VEAL—Noix de veau braisée
> any dry white, modest or
> great wines

OSSO BUCCO
> Chianti classico

PAUPIETTES OF VEAL— Paupiettes de veau
> whites—Alsace, Rully;
> Saint-Emilion, Bourgueil,
> Givry

BREAST OF VEAL—Poitrine de veau
> Languedoc, Minervois, Gard,
> Côtes-du-Rhône reds,
> Gaillac

VEAL SWEETBREADS—Ris de veau
> Médoc,
> Volnay, Pommard

VEAL SWEETBREADS A LA CREME—Ris de veau à la crème

> Mercurey,
> Saumur, Champigny,
> Coteaux du Layon,
> Sauternes

VEAL KIDNEYS—Rognons de veau

> Médoc

SAUTE OF VEAL "MARENGO"—Sauté de veau "marengo"

> *(sauce with tomatoes, garlic, crayfish)*
> Riesling, Vouvray

SAUTE OF VEAL WITH OLIVES—Sauté de veau aux olives

Côtes-du-Rhône, Gigondas

SADDLE OF VEAL—Selle de veau

whites—Anjou; rosés;
great red burgundies—
Aloxe-Corton

CALF'S HEAD "GRIBICHE"— Tête de veau "gribiche"

(a cold sauce)
water,
semi-sweet wines—
Montlouis (Vouvray)
cooled rosés

There are many bad wines in the world, and few good vinegars.

C—PORK

1—IN GENERAL

a) ROASTED, GRILLED

Bordeaux, Pomerol,

Volnay, Vosne-Romanée,
Beaune,
Brouilly, Juliénas,
Chinon, Cahors

b) IN SAUCE
Bordeaux, Médoc,
Saint-Emilion,
Santenay, Fleurie

c) BRAISED, SAUTEED
madeira, sherry, Sancerre

d) IN CRUST
Châteauneuf-du-Pape

2—IN PARTICULAR

BRAISED LOIN OF PORK (ORANGE GARNISH)—Carré de porc braisé à l'orange
Côtes-du-Rhône,
Mâcon, Saint-Emilion
Jurançon (semi-sweet)

Joseph Drouhin

SANTENAY

APPELLATION CONTROLÉE

MIS EN BOUTEILLE PAR
JOSEPH DROUHIN
Maison fondée en 1880
NÉGOCIANT A BEAUNE, COTE-D'OR
AUX CELLIERS DES ROIS DE FRANCE ET DES DUCS DE BOURGOGNE

**ROAST SUCKLING PIG—
Cochon de lait rôti**
>semi-sparkling Vouvray,
>Meursault,
>rosé Champagne or blanc de
>blancs;
>red Bordeaux supérieurs,
>Saint-Emilion,
>Beaune, Chambertin

PORK CHOPS—Côtes de porc
>local reds

**GRILLED PORK CHOPS—
Côtes de porc grillées**
>Meursault,
>red Burgundies

**PORK LIVER "BASQUE"—
Foie de porc "basquaise"**
>Bordeaux supérieurs

**PORK LIVER WITH LEMON—
Foie de porc au citron**
>Bourgueil, rosés from the
>Loire

**PORK LIVER WITH ONIONS—
Foie de porc aux oignons**
>red Bordeaux,
>Côtes Canon-Fronsac

**HAM WITH PINEAPPLE—
Jambon aux ananas**
>Coteaux du Layon, Barsac,
>Château-Chalon,

Monbazillac,
Montravel

**BRAISED HAM—Jambon
braisé**
red Burgundies, Beaujolais

**HAM WITH MUSHROOMS—
Jambon aux champignons**
Beaune, noble growths of
Beaujolais (e.g. Morgon)

**HAM WITH CLOVES—Jambon
au clou de girofle**
semi-sweet white Bordeaux,
Château-Chalon,
Champagne,
Graves (red)

**HAM IN A CRUST—Jambon en
croûte**
Champagne

**ORDINARY HAM—Jambon
ordinaire**
light reds—Chianti,
Valpolicella

**HAM IN PORT WINE—Jambon
au porto**
Bordeaux, Saint-Estèphe

**ROAST YORK HAM—Jambon
York rôti**
Côte de Beaune,
Côte de Nuits

PORK TONGUE—Langue de porc

Chinon, Bourgueil
Bardolino

In praise of Burgundy

The Côte de Beaune and the Côte de Nuits together constitute the Côte d'Or, home of the greatest wines in the world, as some would say. Drinking *Chambertin*, Napoleon's favourite, "you'd think you were swallowing little Jesus in velvet breeches."

Musigny: "To drink it, and to pronounce its name, our lips must take the form of a kiss."

Romanée-Saint-Vivant: Fagon, the doctor, prescribed it for his patient, Louis XIV, the Sun-King.

Corton: Charlemagne's vineyard.

Montrachet: "Should be drunk kneeling, and hats off."

Volnay: Naked girls bathed in a fountain of this wine to greet their king, Louis XVI.

Are Burgundies better than Bordeaux? A great musician said: "They are two great virtuosi playing a sonata for piano and violin." They are as inseparable as two pearls in a single crown.

PIG'S FEET—Pieds de porc
dry whites—Pouilly-Fuissé,
Pouilly-Fumé, Beaujolais,
Mâcon; Tavel

**PIG'S FEET WITH GARLIC—
Pieds de porc à l'ail**
Tavel, Lirac rosé (Rhône)

**PORK PATES—Pâtés de
viande de porc**
dry whites—Alsace, Tokay,
Aligoté, Muscadet, Chablis;
light reds—Beaujolais
(*villages* and "growths"),
Mâconnais; reds—from
other countries

**PORK AND CABBAGE
SOUP—Potées au chou**
robust local wines—Madiran,
Côtes-du-Rhône,
Côtes-de-Fronsac

**PORK RILLETTES—Rillettes
de porc**
Loire, Sancerre

Domaine de la Pierre

1974   1974

MOULIN-A-VENT

APPELLATION MOULIN-A-VENT CONTROLÉE

750 ml

FOILLARD Frères, Propriétaire à ROMANÈCHE-THORINS (S-L)
Distribué par : Ets T. DAVID & L. FOILLARD, négociants à St-Georges (Rhône)

ROAST PORK WITH APPLES —Rôti de porc aux pommes
Touraine whites, rosés, semi-sweet Jurançon (southwest), Coteaux du Layon (sweet)

PIG'S HEAD—Tête de porc
beer

There are more old vine-growers than old doctors.

R. Engel

D—CHICKEN

CHICKEN GIBLETS—Abattis
wines used in cooking giblets—Madiran, Beaujolais, Côte de Nuits

CHICKEN A LA DIABLE—
Poulet à la diable
local reds—Dôle du Valais,
Chiroubles

BOUCHEES A LA REINE
(Chicken in pastry shells)
whites—still or semi-
sparkling Vouvray;
semi-sweet whites;
light reds—Graves

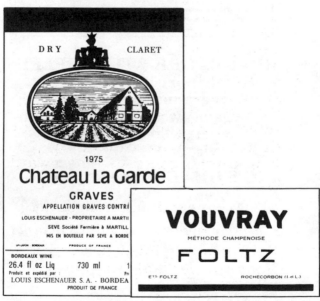

POACHED CAPON—Chapon
poché
Beaujolais,
Pachérenc-du-Vic Bilh,
Côte de Beaune

STUFFED CAPON—Chapon farci

> reds—Côtes de Bordeaux
> Volnay, Monthélie, Rhône;
> Tavel

Wine and its glasses

Champagne is drunk from a tall glass so that we can enjoy the ascending dance of its bubbles. The flat glass is unflattering to this wine, while the flute glass enhances it.

Bordeaux is drunk from a "tulip" glass, elegant and well-bred as the wine itself. Burgundy should be served in a balloon glass smaller at the top, the better to funnel the fumes of this generous wine toward our noses.

Alsace wine is drunk from a long-stemmed glass.

To be avoided: tinted glass, green or amber. We want to see the wine's true color.

CHICKEN "RIESLING"—Coq au "Riesling"

> Alsace

CHICKEN IN WINE SAUCE—
Coq au vin
> Nuits-Saint-Georges;
> preference: Chambertin

CHICKEN IN YELLOW WINE
—Coq au vin jaune
> yellow wine from the Jura

CROQUETTES
> Bordeaux supérieurs—
> Beaune, Bourgueil; white,
> (Clos-des-Mouches);
> Givry

CHICKEN DEMI-DEUIL—
Poularde demi-deuil
> *(garnishes, sauce, truffles)*
> Puligny-Montrachet,
> Beaujolais,
> Vosne-Romanée

MIS EN BOUTEILLE AU CHATEAU

2ᵐᵉ Cru
Classé
en 1855

Nᵒ 31499

73 cl

CHATEAU
RAUSAN-SEGLA
GRAND CRU CLASSÉ
1973 ®

APPELLATION MARGAUX CONTROLÉE

HOLT FRÈRES & FILS, PROPRIÉTAIRES A MARGAUX (GIRONDE)
SOCIÉTÉ FERMIÈRE ET DISTRIBUTEUR EXCLUSIF
LOUIS ESCHENAUER, S.A. - BORDEAUX (GIRONDE)

MARQUE ET BOUTEILLE DÉPOSÉES   PRODUCE OF FRANCE

BORDEAUX WINE		VIN DE BORDEAUX
26.4 fl oz Liq	730 ml	12% alc./vol.
Expédié par :		Shipped by :
Louis ESCHENAUER S.A. NÉGOCIANT-ÉLEVEUR - BORDEAUX (FRANCE)

PRODUIT DE FRANCE   a/76

TURKEY—Dinde
   Moulis, great growths of
   Saint-Julien,
   Pomerol,
   Nuits-Saint-Georges,
   Châteauneuf-du-Pape

STUFFED TURKEY—Dinde farcie
   (truffles, chestnuts)
   Médoc, great growths
   (Château-Lafite,
   Château-Latour),

**Château-Cheval-Blanc,
Corton-Grancey,
Romanée-Conti,
Clos-de-Bèze**

FRICASSEE
Aligoté, white Graves,
Condrieu

PRODUIT FRANÇAIS   PRODUCE OF FRANCE

Mis en Bouteilles à F. 33480 - 297 par :

DOURTHE FRÈRES
Fondée en 1840

NÉGOCIANTS A BORDEAUX (GIRONDE) FRANCE

SAINT-JULIEN

APPELLATION CONTROLÉE

73cl

730 ml   11% alc./vol.
VIN DE TABLE ROUGE   RED TABLE WINE

POULE-AU-POT
*(pot-au-feu with beef and
stuffed chicken)*
Médoc, Graves,
Côte de Beaune, Mercurey

CHICKEN WITH ALMONDS—
Poulet aux amandes
Provence rosés,
rosés from Béarn,
Meursault, Pouilly-Fuissé,
red Graves, Saint-Emilion,
Côtes-du-Rhône

CHICKEN WITH PINEAPPLE
—Poulet à l'ananas
Anjou, Tavel,
Sauternes

CHICKEN, BASQUE STYLE
—Poulet basquaise
(béchamel)
Irouléguy (south-west
France),
Vins des Sables,
dry or semi-sweet whites

CHICKEN ON THE SPIT—
Poulet à la broche
red Arbois or Sauternes

CHICKEN CHASSEUR—
Poulet chasseur
(garnish of sautéed
mushrooms, shallots)
great full-bodied red wines,
red Graves,
semi-sweet white wines

CHICKEN CASSEROLE— Poulet en cocotte
(bacon, onions)
Bergerac, Listrac, Moulis

CHICKEN PAPRIKA—Poulet au paprika
Rhône, Châteauneuf-du-Pape;
Badacsonyi,
Egri Bikaver (Hungary)

FRIED CHICKEN—Poulet frit à l'américaine
Bordeaux Supérieurs,
Listel gris (rosé),
Saumur

ROAST CHICKEN AND FRENCH FRIES—Poulet rôti aux frites
Beaujolais

CHICKEN IN GRAVY—Poulet en sauce

dry whites, rosés from the Loire, reds, Saint-Estèphe, Hermitage

CHICKEN SUPREME— Suprême de volaille

white bordeaux, Châteaux de Pauillac, Saint-Amour

TERRINE OF CHICKEN LIVER—Terrine de foie de volaille

> robust whites, Burgundies, or reds—Condrieu, Moulin-à-vent

E—GOOSE AND DUCK

1—IN GENERAL

a) ROASTED

> Côtes-de-Fronsac
> Nuits-Saint-Georges,
> Pommard, Côte-Rôtie,
> Beaune,

Tavel, Jura,
Châteauneuf-du-Pape,
Chianti,
California Zinfandel

b) IN SAUCE
Saint-Emilion, Pomerol,
Corton, Musigny,
Ermitage, Mâcon, Saumur,
Riesling, Rhine, Mosel

c) GOOSE
Médoc

d) DUCK
Ermitage

In praise of Bordeaux

The charm and feminine virtues of this region would lead us to refer to it as a great lady, rather than a lord. Bordeaux is a "she," and Burgundy a "he," or so the experts have said over the years.

The poets have gone them one better by referring to the "classic grace" of the wines of Bordeaux, comparable to the verse of Racine. The poet Ausone, who was born and who died in Bordeaux, left his name to one of the first classified *grands crus* of Saint-Emilion: Château-Ausone. François Villon also sang the praises of Saint-Emilion, the "god-daughter of Bordeaux":

> Of that elect I wish to be
> That drink it in eternity.

The choicest region for Bordeaux, Médoc, "is a green oasis. Blanketed with vines divided by a thousand paths, fair to the eyes of poet and tippler alike."

2—IN PARTICULAR

BALLOTTINE OF DUCKLING —Ballottine de canard

red Graves, Mâcon,
Champigny,
Châteauneuf-du-Pape,
Bâtard-Montrachet,

DUCK WITH PINEAPPLE— Canard à l'ananas

Corton-Charlemagne,
Fronsac, Sauternes

BRAISED DUCK IN WHITE WINE—Canard braisé au vin blanc

champagne blanc de blancs,
sparkling white (brut or very
dry)

DUCK WITH OLIVES—Canard aux olives
> Médoc

DUCK A L'ORANGE—Canard à l'orange
> Bordeaux Supérieurs,
> Côte de Beaune, Sauternes,
> Alsace wines, natural sweet
> wines—Banyuls,
> Muscat de Mireval,
> Muscat de Rivesaltes,
> Cabernet d'Anjou,
> Château-Chalon,
> Clairette du Languedoc,
> Rancio (aged in the sun)

CASSOULET OF DUCK— Cassoulet
> *(preserved duck, white beans, pork, mutton)*
> Saint-Emilion,
> Côtes-du-Rhône,
> Brouilly, Mâcon, Fitou,
> Cahors, Minervois;
> whites—Knipperlé, Zwicker,
> rosé of Anjou, Tavel

CIVET OF GOOSE—Oie en civet
> *(stewed in goose-blood, red wine)*
> Côte-Rotie, Saint-Emilion,
> Nuits, Beaune

PRESERVED GOOSE—Confit d'oie

young Bordeaux (tannic),
Alsatian Tokay

I love these old wines that die in an odour of sanctity.

P. Poupon

F—LAMB AND MUTTON
1—IN GENERAL
preference: Pauillac

a) ROASTED, GRILLED
Saint-Emilion, Fronsac,
Pommard, Santenay, Corton,
Gigondas, Ermitage,
Côtes-du-Rhône

b) IN SAUCE
Médoc, Pomerol,
Volnay, Vosne-Romanée,
Montrachet, Fleurie,
Bourgueil

2—IN PARTICULAR

LAMB—Agneau
Médoc, Graves,
Côte de Beaune,
Tavel, Bourgueil, Jura;
whites—Saumur, Riesling,
Mâcon

**OVEN-ROASTED SUCKLING
LAMB—Agneau de lait au four**
Provence rosés, Corbières,
Ermitage, Côtes Bordeaux,
Santenay, Vouvray

**CURRIED LAMB—Agneau à
l'indienne**
Provence rosés,
white Ermitage,
Arbois, Château-Chalon,
Châteauneuf-du-Pape

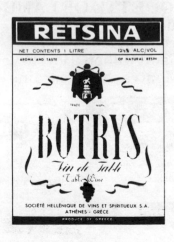

LAMB, GREEK STYLE—
Agneau à la grecque
(garlic, lemon, flour)
water, rosés, Retsina

LAMB, MOROCCAN STYLE—
Agneau à la marocaine
(vinegar, mint)
mint tea,
Pauillac,
Mascara (Algeria)

BARON OF LAMB—Baron
d'agneau
(roast saddle or leg)
Bordeaux, Saint-Julien,
Pauillac, Côtes-du-Rhône,
Coteaux du Tricastin,
Châteauneuf-du-Pape,
Rioja

BLANQUETTE OF LAMB—
Blanquette d'agneau
(stewed in white sauce)
Saint-Julien, Beychevelle,
Montrachet, Touraine

SKEWERED LAMB (IRANIAN STYLE)—Brochette à l'iranienne

(olive oil, tomatoes)

Saint-Estèphe,
rosés from Provence,
Rioja,
Amarone (recioto della
Valpolicella), Barbaresco

CARRE OF LAMB—Carré d'agneau

Côtes-du-Rhône,
Saint-Nicolas-de-Bourgueil,
Saint-Julien

LAMB'S BRAINS—Cervelle d'agneau

Sancerre, rosés of Anjou,
Chinon red

LAMB CHOPS—Côtelettes d'agneau

Bordeaux, Côtes-de-Bourg,
Graves (red), Pomerol,
Mercurey,
Tavel, Frascati (white),
Californian Merlot

COUSCOUS

mint tea,
Mascara, Pauillac, Chusclan,
Provence rosés, young red
wines

**VALLE
VERMIGLIA**

WHITE WINE - VIN BLANC
FRASCATI
Superiore

DENOMINAZIONE DI ORIGINE CONTROLLATA

PRODUCED AND BOTTLED IN THE PRODUCTION ZONE BY
PRODUIT ET MIS EN BOUTEILLE DANS LA ZONE DE PRODUCTION PAR
VINI VALLE VERMIGLIA S.p.A.

FRASCATI - ITALIE

720 ml   ALC./VOL. 12 %

Reg. Imb. 1715 Roma

CURRIED MUTTON—Curry de mouton

>   Bordeaux supérieurs,
>   Crozes-Hermitage (red),
>   Cornas, Tavel

BURGUNDY: THE VINEYARDS

Burgundy extends some 200 km.
from Dijon to Lyon, and includes
the vineyards of Chablis, the Côte
d'Or, the Côte chalonnaise, Mâcon
and Beaujolais. The main vine-
plants are Pinot noir, Chardonnay,
Gamay and Aligoté.

Burgundy wines are full-bodied, robust, with a pronounced bouquet, and need to be aged. The whites of the region are equally sturdy, pale-gold in color with a tinge of green, and can also be kept for aging.

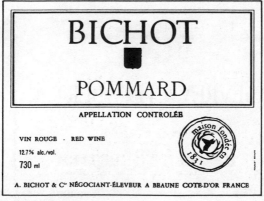

LEG OF LAMB—Gigot d'agneau
(elaborate preparation)
Médoc (noble growths):
Château-Montrose,
Château-Calon-Ségur,
Château-Pontet-Canet;
Aloxe-Corton, Pommard,
Bouzy (still red wine from
Champagne)
Châteauneuf-du-Pape,
Brunello (Italian)

IRISH STEW
beer

MOUSSAKA
(ground meat, egg plant)
Beaujolais, Brouilly,
Moulin-à-Vent, Chianti,
California Burgundy,
Boutari

B&G
FONDÉE EN 1725

GEVREY-CHAMBERTIN

APPELLATION GEVREY CHAMBERTIN CONTROLEE

VIN ROUGE   RED WINE

EMBOUTEILLE PAR/BOTTLED BY

BARTON & GUESTIER
NÉGOCIANTS – ÉLEVEURS A BLANQUEFORT – FRANCE

750 ml   12% alc./vol.

MUTTON CHOP
    Moulin-à-Vent, Hermitage

KIDNEYS—Rognons
    Bordeaux supérieurs,
    Champagne,
    Côte de Nuits,
    Gevrey-Chambertin

LAMB SAUTE—Sauté d'agneau
    Saint-Estèphe,
    Beaujolais-Villages,
    Beaujolais

SADDLE OF LAMB—Selle d'agneau
    Burgundy,
    Chambolle-Musigny,
    Clos-de-Vougeot, Brouilly,
    Château-Pétrus (Pomerol)

My belly full, my soul is stout:
Disaster can not put me out!
           Molière

G—GAME

I. FURRED GAME

1—IN GENERAL
very robust wines,
preferably Burgundies

a) Roasted
Saint-Emilion, Pomerol,
Côte de Nuits,
Châteauneuf-du-Pape

b) In Sauce
Pomerol, Musigny,
Bonnes-Mares,
Chambolle-Musigny,
Romanée-Conti, Gigondas

*I'm not a fussy man. I'm quite satisfied
with the best.*
Churchill

2—IN PARTICULAR

VENISON—Chevreuil
Pommard, Côte-Rotie,
Saint-Estèphe;
preference: Clos-de-Vougeot

**HAUNCH OF VENISON—
Gigue de chevreuil**
(pepper sauce)
robust reds,
Côtes-du-Rhône,
Hermitage

**NOISETTE OF VENISON
ROMANOFF—Noisette de
Chevreuil Romanov**
(cucumbers, mushrooms)
Pommard,
Châteauneuf-du-Pape,
Cornas, Volnay

RABBIT—Lapin
Beaujolais, white Anjou,
local wines, Côtes du
Lubéron, Ventoux

**RABBIT, MUSTARD SAUCE—
Lapin à la moutarde**
local reds, Cahors, Madiran,
Beaujolais, Moulin-à-Vent

**CARBONNADE OF RABBIT—
Carbonnade de lapin**
beer,
rosé wines,
local red wines

ROAST HARE—Lièvre rôti
    Côtes-du-Rhône, Ermitage,
    Châteauneuf-du-Pape,
    Graves (red),
    whites—Pouilly-Fumé,
    semi-sweet Alsatian

JUGGED HARE—Lièvre en civet
    (blood of the animal)
        Beaujolais, noble growths:
        Morgon, Juliénas, Chenas,
        Fleurie;
        Rhône, Saint-Emilion,
        Pomerol,

Graves (red),
Côte de Nuits,
Côte de Beaune,
Mâcon, Cahors

SADDLE OF HARE GRAND VENEUR—Râble de lièvre grand veneur

(brown game sauce, hare's blood, pepper)
Pomerol, Saint-Estèphe,
Pommard, Barolo,
Gattinara (Italian)

MOOSE, BEAR—Orignal, ours
>Côte de Nuits,
>Saint-Emilion, great Médoc
>wines—Saint-Julien;
>Côte-Rôtie,
>Châteauneuf-du-Pape,
>South African Cabernet,
>California Cabernet,
>white German wines

II. FEATHERED GAME

1—IN GENERAL
>rich, mellow, light wines;
>preference: Bordeaux

a) WOODCOCK, THRUSH, LARK
>Pomerol,
>Corton, Pommard,
>Hermitage,
>Valpolicella

b) WILD DUCK, PHEASANT, PARTRIDGE
>Morgon, Château-Haut-Brion,
>Graves—Saint-Estèphe,
>Saint-Julien,
>Musigny, Chambertin,
>Cornas

Château
LÉOVILLE BARTON
CRU CLASSÉ EN 1855

APPELLATION St JULIEN CONTRÔLÉE

PROPRIÉTAIRE · SOCIÉTÉ CIVILE AGRICOLE
DES CHATEAUX LANGOA ET LÉOVILLE BARTON

MIS EN BOUTEILLE AU CHÂTEAU

VIN ROUGE — PRODUIT DE FRANCE / PRODUCE OF FRANCE — RED WINE
730 ml — INTERNATIONAL WINES & SPIRITS Ltd. 12° alc./vol.
MONTREAL CANADA

*Every man at the beginning
doth set forth good wine,
and when men have well drunk,
then that which is worse:
but thou has kept the good
wine until now.*
John II, 10.

2—IN PARTICULAR

WOODCOCK—Bécasses
Chambertin,
Chambolle-Musigny,
Richebourg,
Nuits-Saint-Georges,
Pommard

WOODCOCK PIE—Bécasses en croûte
Châteauneuf-du-Pape

QUAIL—Cailles
Bordeaux, Graves (red),
Beaujolais,
Johannesberg Riesling
(New York)

QUAIL—Cailles
(served cold)
still white Anjou,
white Beaujolais, Tavel

SKEWERED QUAIL—Caille en brochette
Côtes de Provence

ROAST QUAIL WITH GRAPES—Cailles rôties au raisin
Saint-Julien, Sauternes

STUFFED QUAIL—Cailles farcies
Médoc, Bourgueil,
Cabernet Sauvignon
(California)

WILD DUCK—Canard
robust reds, classified
growths of Médoc,
Saint-Emilion,
Californian Cabernet,
Côte de Nuits,
Côte-Rotie,
semi-sweet Rhine wines

WILD DUCK A L'ORANGE— Canard à l'orange
Chambertin,
Château-Chalon,
sherry

THE VINEYARDS OF BORDEAUX

The region of the Châteaux (no less than 1500 of them) includes the vineyards of Médoc, Graves, Saint-Emilion, Pomerol, Sauternes and

Entre-Deux-Mers. The main vine-plants used are Cabernet, Sauvignon, Sémillon, Merlot, Muscadelle, Verdot and Malbec. The communes of Médoc mentioned most frequently in this book are Saint-Estèphe, Pauillac, Saint-Julien, Moulis, Margaux, i.e., those with the best vineyards or Châteaux, such as Lafite, Margaux, Latour, Mouton-Rothschild.

Saint-Emilion and Pomerol also have great vineyards: Ausone, Figeac, Trottevieille, Pétrus.

PHEASANT BRAISED WITH CIDER AND APPLES—Faisan braisé au cidre et aux pommes

    cider, Champagne, sparkling wine from the Loire

PHEASANT PROVENCALE—Faisan à la provençale

    Champagne

PHEASANT RAGOUT—Faisan en salmis

    great Burgundies, red Hermitage, Chianti Classico, Napa Cabernet

ROAST PHEASANT—Faisan rôti
> Cahors, Corbières,
> Chambertin,
> Alsatian,
> Tavel

BALLOTTINE OF PHEASANT —faisan en ballottine
> white wine from the Loire,
> Bordeaux supérieurs

THRUSH—Grives
> Pommard,
> Châteauneuf-du-Pape

THRUSH PIE—Grives en croûte
> Arbois (red),
> Champagne

ROAST PARTRIDGE SOUWAROFF—Perdreau Souvarov rôti
(foie gras, truffles)
> Château-Margaux,
> Clos-de-Vougeot, Corton,
> Pommard, Rhône,
> Côte-Rôtie

PARTRIDGE—Perdrix
(older birds)
> Saint-Emilion, Corton, Nuits,
> Rhône, Saint-Estèphe

PARTRIDGES WITH CABBAGE—Perdrix aux chou
Burgundy, Ermitage,
Arbois (red),
Alsatian,
Muscadet, Sancerre

PIGEON CASSEROLE—Pigeon en cocotte
whites—Alsatian,

Pouilly-Fuissé,
Muscadet;
reds—Beaujolais, Mâcon,
Côtes-du-Rhône, Fitou,
Merlot (California)

ROAST PIGEON—Pigeon rôti
Pomerol

VII. CHEESE

Oh, how excellent is Chambertin with Roquefort cheese to reanimate our love! And to bring to precocious maturity a love just born!
Casanova

1. GOAT CHEESE—Chèvre
(example: Crottin de Chavignol)
dry whites—Loire, Sancerre, Pouilly-Fuissé
rich, fruity reds, rosés

2. FROM COW'S MILK—Vache

a) velvety crust, fermented, soft centre
(examples: Brie, Camembert, Carré de l'est, Saint-Marcellin)
Graves (red),
Château-Haut-Brion,
Pomerol,
Saint-Emilion (châteaux),

Corton, Beaune, Pommard,
Chambertin, Richebourg,
Vougeot, Morgon, Bouzy,
port

b) smooth crust, soft centre
   *(examples: Pont-l'Evêque,
   Maroilles, Munster, Vacherin)*
      Corton, Côte-Rôtie,
      Châteauneuf-du-Pape,
      Barolo, Ghemme;
      N.B.: with Munster cheese, a
      preference to
      Gewürztraminer or Bual
      (Madeira)

c) hard, firm, dry cheese
*(examples: Gruyère,
Emmenthal, Cheddar, Edam,
Stilton)*
robust reds—Corton, Volnay,
Romanée, Santenay,
Médoc (second or third
growths),
dry whites—Alsatian,
Chablis,
Fendant, Arbois, Soave

d) uncooked cheese (pressed)
*(examples: Saint-Paulin,
Port-Salut, Tomme, Saint-
Nectaire, Oka, Gouda,
Reblochon, Cantal)*
dry whites and rosés, fruity,
light—Graves, Pomerol,
Fleurie, Arbois

e) blue cheese (semi-soft)
(examples: Auvergne blue, Bresse, Ermite, Gorgonzola)
light reds—Brouilly, Barbera, Bardolino, Dolcetto,
sweet whites—Amabile

f) fresh cheese (non-fermented)
(examples: Petit-Suisse, Double-crème Boursin)
dry whites, or fruity or semi-sweet whites;
sweet rosés

3. FROM EWE'S MILK—Brebis
(examples: Roquefort, Rocamadour)
great red wines—
Château-Haut-Brion;
N.B.: Roquefort (two schools of thought)
1—Chambertin
2—Sauternes

VIII. DESSERTS AND SWEETS

Good food and fine wine make paradise on earth.
Henri IV

APRICOTS CONDE—Abricots Condé

    water,
    rosés—Monbazillac (sweet),
    Madeira, Tawny Port,
    Hungarian Tokay

APRICOTS AU FOUR

    water,
    Frontignan (muscat),
    Quarts-de-Chaume,
    Sauternes

APRICOTS AU KIRSCH

    water,
    Kirsch,
    Moscato d'Asti Spumante

PINEAPPLE—Ananas
Chartreuse, sherry (sweet),
apricot brandy

RUM BABA—Baba au rhum
water,
Monbazillac,
Martinique punch

BANANAS FLAMBE—
Bananes flambées
water,
punch,
semi-sweet whites,
Cointreau,
Anisette

IN PRAISE OF CHAMPAGNE

Champagne, the wine of feasts and rejoicing, is unique not only in its elegance, its aerial quality and its clarity; it differs from other wines also in its lack of respect for the laws that rule the others. It obeys itself alone. The "king of wines"—who'd have thought it?—is blended! And this is precisely the secret of its greatness.

The overweening merit of Dom Pérignon is not that he established the rules for catching the sparkle in a bottle, nor that he revived the use of the cork—forgotten since Roman times—but that he thought of mixing wines from the Marne, the Aisne and the Aube. In our own time, the *chef de cave* of a Champagne maker must choose among fifty to fifty-six growths out of the 250-odd Champagne growths in order to create, year after year, the Champagne that maintains the reputation of his label.

Champagne is the only wine that makes the woman who drinks it lovelier. It makes her eyes shine without bringing a flush to her cheeks!

**APPLE FRITTERS—Beignets
aux pommes**
water, cider,
sweet white wines

CHERRIES—Cerises
Curaçao, Cointreau

CRÊPE SUZETTE
   sweet whites—Vouvray,
   Asti Spumante,
   dry Champagne,
   Château-d'Yquem

DATES—Dattes
   Anisette, Cointreau,
   Prunelle

STRAWBERRIES—Fraises
   Madeira, port (tawny),
   Muscatelle,
   Hungarian Tokay,
   Benedictine, Vieille Cure

**STRAWBERRIES AND
CREAM—Fraises à la crème**
   sweet, white Bordeaux

RASPBERRIES—Framboises
   Chartreuse, sherry

FRUITS

a) Acid
   (oranges, lemons, grapefruit)
   water

b) Others
   Monbazillac, Anjou, Vouvray,
   Muscat, Banyuls, Port,
   Madeira, Marsala,
   Champagne (brut or extra-
   dry)

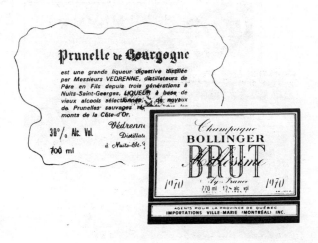

CAKE—Gâteau
Asti Spumante,
Madeira (Malmsey),
cream sherry

RICE CAKE—Gâteau de riz
Loire, Sancerre

MELON
Sauternes, port

CHOCOLATE MOUSSE—
Mousse au chocolat
water

NUTS—Noix
port, sherry

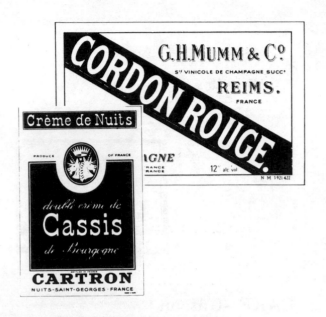

PASTRIES AND CREAMS—
Pâtisserie et crèmes
Vin de Paille (Jura),
muscats from Roussillon,
Samos,
Sauternes

PEACHES AND WINE—
Pêches au vin
Beaujolais, Juliénas

PEARS—Poires
No particular wine. If it must
be, then Asti or Cassis
(liqueur), Crème de Cacao

ROAST APPLES—Pommes au four

Bordeaux, Saint-Emilion

PUDDING

Clairette de Die,
Loire, Pouilly-Fumé

GRAPES—Raisin

No wine. If it must be, then
Asti or Prunelle

FRUIT SALADS—Salades de fruits

water

**SHERBETS AND ICE CREAM
—Sorbets et glaces**
  water

SOUFFLES—Soufflés
  Vouvray, Coteaux du Layon
  California white Riesling

SOUFFLE GRAND MARNIER
  Champagne (brut)

**APPLE PIE—Tarte aux
pommes**
  German wines

**RASPBERRY PIE—Tarte aux
framboises**
  Anjou

PLUM PIE—Tarte aux prunes
  Barsac, Monbazillac,
  Sauternes

COFFEE AND ...

After the meal we normally move to the living room. In other days, the men herded themselves off to enjoy a port and a cigar and discreetly exchange remarks of no interest to the ladies. This custom has happily fallen into disuse, and we now drink our coffee together.

This is the moment for passing around the cognac, the pause after a good dinner. In a balloon glass, or in tiny liqueur glasses, as some brandy-makers recommend. Or what about an Armagnac? Or perhaps a fine white schnapps such as Mirabelle or Quetsche? Your wish is my command.

And to your very good health!

Now that we've drunk well, eaten well ... isn't life good, Madame? No reply? What are you dreaming about as you watch your cigarette smoke curl toward the lamp?

Pierre Petel
Montreal

135

APPENDIX:

THE FLAVORS OF WINES

The word "flavor" sums up all the sensations of smell and taste that we receive from a wine. The tongue and the palate can distinguish only a limited number of tastes, and it is the olfactory stimulations, especially those that rise from inside the mouth to the nasal cavity, that define the true nuances between wines.

The following is a list of 60 wines and their respective flavors, which I would ask the reader not to consider as absolute. In wine-tasting as in other things subjectivity plays its role. Without taking the list too literally, then, let us think of it as an exercise, or a guide to a general appreciation that may allow us to reach a better discernment of the tastes and aromas of our wines.

Amarone: raisins
Arbois: raspberries, truffles
White Arbois: walnut leaves, gun flint
Barolo: spices
Béarn: carnations, cloves
Beaujolais: strawberries
Bordeaux: black currants, spices, pine, cigar-box wood
Burgundy: spruce gum, violets, truffles
Bourgueil: raspberries
Brouilly: peonies, plums
Chablis: mineral perfume, stone, cut hay
Corton-Charlemagne: fresh almonds, grilled nuts, truffles, cinnamon
Coteaux-du-Layon: apples
Châteauneuf-du-Pape: iodine, raspberries, burnt smell, spices
Chinon: violets
Condrieu: peaches, apricots, roses
Cabernet-Sauvignon: cedar, tar, violet, lilacs
Cabernet franc: raspberries
Chianti: violets
Corvo: apricots, figs
Côte-Rotie: violets, spices
Costières-du-Gard: ginger
Chardonnay: apples, ripe bananas
Château-Grillet (white): apricots, flowers, musk
Côtes-du-Rhône: grenadine syrup
Dolcetto d'Alba: liquorice
Gamay: strawberry, ripe bananas
Hermitage: mulberries, egg plant
Fendant: beer
Fleurie: réséda, iris, violets, musk
German wines: Spring flowers, pears (Mosel), peaches, honey, jonquils
Graves: vanilla
Gevrey-Chambertin: liquorice

Juliénas: peaches, raspberries
Meursault: oats, hazel-nuts
Montrachet: peaches, apricots, truffles, honey
Morgon: apricots, red currants, kirsch, cherries
Muscadet: apples, musk
Musigny: violets, almonds
Nuits-Saint-Georges: old leather
Orvieto: ripe fruit
Pouilly-Fumé: almond flowers, smoked pork, gun flint, spices
Pommard: pepper
Piemont: liquorice, spices
Pinot noir: black currants
Port: strawberries, dried figs
Rosés of Provence: grenadine, vanilla, black currants, raspberries
Puligny-Montrachet: ferns
Riesling: musk, cinnamon
Rioja: liquorice
Sherry: flavour of bread or yeast, walnut leaves
Sancerre: gun flint, old cognac
Savoie: apples
Saint-Amour: peaches, réséda
Soave: bitter almonds
Sylvaner: flint, hawthorn
Tavel: flowers, wild strawberries
Traminer: faded roses, violets
Vosne-Romanée: humus, underbrush, dead leaves, violets
Vougeot: truffles

INDEX

D

Wine-tasting Notes

_____

_____

_____

_____

_____

_____

_____

_____

_____

_____

_____

_____

_____

_____

Wine-tasting Notes

_____

_____

_____

_____

_____

_____

_____

_____

_____

_____

_____

_____

_____

_____

By the same author:

Aie! Aie! Aie! (Ferron Éditeur) Poemes
Il n'y a plus d'Indiens a Hochelaga (Ferron Éditeur) Poemes
Le Vin (Éditions de l'Homme)
Vins pour cent recettes (Éditions La Presse)
Guide du week-end (Éditions La Presse)
Deux pionniers bavardent (Fides)
Entre deux vins (Éditions du Jour)

In preparation:

L'Arbre de l'Oiseveté (Leméac)